PAPERCUTS LEAVES MARKS

Nidhi Shah

Writer's Pocket

First published by Writer's Pocket in 2021

email: publish@writerspocket.com

cover design by Janhvi Kriplani

ISBN-13: 978-93-6083-503-3

www.writerspocket.com

There are some spaces,
Pieces, only filled by the one
Like a puzzle to be made,
There's only one that fits the role
But the picture will never be complete,
The pieces will come and go,
You'll come across some misfits
And you'll have a tough time letting them go
But set them free as you may,
They're the ladder to your growth,
Because even one missing piece
And it's a whole different puzzle.

we make stars of the people we see at night,
sparkling above us like they never died
to be so close but not enough,
there are miles between us
we would never cross.

The enormity of our minds
Lays in the undertone of what we speak,
Every syllable has an echo
And it travels as far as we please.
Our speech dictates to our destiny
To which we are to bow down,
It's woven by our words,
Hardly written at all.

What makes you has made the universe;
Between cosmic oceans and your being,
It hasn't left out an ounce of greatness.

The love we lack is the love taken away from us.

There are people who have lived long without love and even longer with hate.

The hate, it consumes you,
So you don't think about how hollow you've become.
That flowery world of yours will whirl back into the ground
To rekindle its mortality,
While you,
You just wait for the sombres to creep in.

You are in all shades of blue I've never seen,
Sometimes as light as his eyes
And sometimes as deep as the sapphires.

As you grow old, you get stronger,
You crash against the boulders with one loud thud
And then you're back again for another fight.

Surpass the limit of what anyone thinks of you.

No victory but you're not defeated,
Your battle will always be the most magnificent one,
The one in which you bleed in blue.

They are all around us, all kinds. They let go of our bad and hold on so tight to our bare good. They make space for us when we reek of cigarettes and pain. They feed on our skin till we become one of them.

The facade we carry is the work of a thousand tears that have been tormenting us since time.

The face they mirror is the mask we too shall get.

It leaves no one.

You try to get me and I try to be you.
It's the love at its strongest,
It's the love the world needs,
And it's the love that heals.
You burn so I breathe and you shield so I survive.
Ma, I'm lost without you and found by your light,
Hardly enough without you but whole by your side.

Eyes wide open, there's a body there,
No tears, no grief,
Nobody's there.
Few words in the air that should have been said
Or just a faint smile for the one that lived.
No guilt, no remorse,
Nobody's there,
Even the soul left just a body there.

Our parents didn't know better,
Otherwise they would have sat by us.
Our trauma was a compulsion,
In order to be in hands with the world
And I'm glad they didn't keep me a soft sampling,
Even unintentionally, I was in the wilderness and thriving.

Give up.
Give it up.
The constant need to undo
Dragging that heavy heart full of regret,
Holding on to what reduces you,
Self loathing everything,
Give it all up.
But that life you have,
You own every breath of it,
Don’t spare it for how miserable it makes you.

The day we call ourselves broken,
Is when we unite with the rest,
The pieces that scattered
Are indeed picked up by someone else,
You are made of the fragments you lifted
Of people who think you are gifted,
The whole of you is most of them
And it's then you realise,
Breaking is not so bad.

A rose for everyday I can't see you
And I'll have a garden blooming of red.
The scent,
The fragrance,
It numbs the pain but those thorns,
They poke and sometimes we even bleed,
But it's never enough to drain the life out of us
So I wait for tomorrow, another day
Where there'll be another story
And another rose.

When our hearts are to be ripped apart
For the grieving sake
Of a fresh start,
I'll stage my support,
I'll leave with a smile
But
What after goodbye
What good a word
Has it ever been enough
To part two raging souls
That'll be enough today
To take away,
My longing love.

Four walls with no windows,
Dark and hollow,
Nobody gets out because they can't.
The times they hustle to leave,
A part of them is always sulking in that only corner.
The same thoughts that reek of despair on a reel,
Each time it gets heavier,
They get visions of their happier times
And watch them get darker.
They are bodies wondering,
Searching for their souls,
They collide into each other
But not one say of pain.

They've forgotten how to feel or once they've felt
greater pains, which makes them so numb today.

My heart aches
When my eyes see
You two living my dream,
My fingers tremble
When my mind wanders
To places you've been
Not with me.
You are living the story I couldn’t complete,
Chained to the ground,
Being a spectator,
You are making me watch something
I couldn't forgive myself for seeing.

A few thousand thoughts
Don't tell me to stop
For if I could, I would.

They kill in silence
With a knife so sharp,
Slow but they let it flow.

With ease, they invade
Till enough is endured.

Tonight wasn't the last fight.

If you've ever loved them, you still do.
It's the love with no spark, lacking passion, in the most disconnected way.
Your heart doesn't pound when you see them, no goose bumps, no butterflies.
The love is dead but it's still there.
You remember them in their old flesh but can't feel for the person they've become.
The time spent together could have been so honest but you wouldn't do it again.

You simply watch them your whole life with the eyes of a bare spectator.
Unattached but it's still there.

There is a myth in the mist,
Carried by the breeze,
A much told truth,
That remained hard to please.

They said leave when the love does but how do we leave our loved ones?

It estranged two souls
Made in the temple of the lord,
Who disobeyed the greater bargain
To uphold their fleeting vows.

What would you do
If I told you
That I woke up to
Not loving you?

Would the day even end,
Will the night sky fall,
How do I look into your eyes
And say it all?

I can be hurt
But not the one hurting.
Is our life so small
That we even stop breathing?

Would the pain even end
Will you ever forgive me,
How do I look ahead,
Leaving behind all our memories?

A serenade of sirens, 2020

Another ambulance today,
Much closer to my house
Than it was yesterday.
I saw them take her away,
Her hand hanging from the stretcher,
She didn't move at it all
And in the same stillness, she left.

The crowd got thinner,
A few moved around the corner,
It was that time again,
Another siren getting louder.

Even your today is too far gone,
To live yesterday is a tragedy,
If you belonged you would be there,
But you were taken.

Even the start to a finer life may seem like continued devastation from previous chapters but that's hardly it.

Something fell apart *because* something was falling in place.

A few odd days
When you fail to believe,
You will still have my shoulders
For your pain to relieve.

You'll feel much lesser then
Lesser of the wrong kind.
The world is not so evil,
It gives you if you find.

My faith lies in you,
So when you shake,
My pillars tremble too,
Just hold my hand then
So we can sail through.

When we part our ways,
If we ever do,
I'll be at the end of the tunnel,
I'll be there for you.

All it takes is one glance at a picture, what was once a moment is now a memory. A faint one, perhaps. It brings back the laughter, the feelings, the time just to realize how much has changed ever since. They said, “I love you forever,” and how they say that to other people. Forever is more of an illusion than a lie, an illusion we all think we have a hold of until we don’t.

When her eyes look away,
Do you follow the trail?
The fall upon the room's mere detail,
They hide beneath the ordinary,
The run from the chase,
Your eyes,
So captivating,
She'll clench on her freedom
Before she drowns in them.

When I see you from a distance,
I see the blinding glow.
You take over me
And I lose control.
If I came close,
Would you ever know?

I feel your celestial aura
So pure for this human soul,
I can't amount to what you are,
May your divinity grace us all.

All they want
Is a familiar life,
The one they know
Is tainted
With agonizing memories
That haunt them.

The one they had
Was true it’s spine,
Enough in all ways
And once in a lifetime.

You can feed
On the leftovers,
Of the love
That left you
On a dark night,
The moon will phase out
And you will still be knocking
On the same door
That lead you
To your despair.

City lights try to
Tame the shine
Of what burns bright
From a thousand miles.

We keep visiting our memories
Because it's a better place to be at
Than the bitter present itself,
We keep them near
But not too close,
We are confined to visit
And out of bounds to relive it.

You say it's easier
When the heart stops beating
And the eyes slowly close.
You pray,
Not for an eternal life
But an early death.
You stay
And watch us
Blossom on your barren land
And you ponder,
Why couldn't you do the same.

In sickness and in health,
You were promised the world
But I walked out of it
Not long ago,
Broke my vows
Before I broke your home,
Should have stayed
But I left you all alone.
You, you rise again
Like the phoenix you are
And I'll fall back
On my next doomed love.

Loneliness comes in waves
When you sleep
Each night
To the thought of that person
And wake up
Every morning
In an empty bed.

You've been burnt
By your dark infernos
In silhouettes of love,
It took the body of a stranger,
The match that lit you
Started a wildfire,
So young a face,
It walked you down your pyre.

To know what you did
Or keep wondering,
It doesn't get easier.
I see them knowing the truth
And I see you living with it,
Each day, you're less of yourself,
It's wearing you down
And leaving you to shreds.

Perhaps, I don't know it because it is not in me to shoulder your pain.

The thought alone of seeing you
After all this time has passed
Is enough for me to know
Why we didn't last.

We had it beautiful
Till we put it a box,
Nobody gets in, nobody gets out.

Shared the same air
Till only crumbs
Which would never suffice
For the love that deranged.

It's the sound that rings
Hollow in your ears
of the voices
Trying to reach you.
When the moonless night
Comes for you,
They'll come to life
In honor to avenge you.

They are made of glass,
Some hearts we meet.
Fragile yet unbreakable
Because nobody would dare to.
You can see through them
But can't fathom what they behold.
If you get to hold them,
You must be chosen.
But be careful,
They are your once in a lifetime,
If they fall,
Only you shatter.

It's a Sunday
And I see you work,
Privileged enough to not see what it takes,
Like a wall, you stand before us,
Even the ungodly won't break your strength,
You carved a life so beautiful
And gave it in my hands.
There is nothing I know of struggle,
Not half of what you've lived,
There is a world that scares you
But you've raised to get the best of it,
You've given me so much
That it's only fair to think
You wrote my fate.

In my grief, I am asking you,
Do not return.
The day I put you beneath me,
Promise me to remain there.
The house you left,
Don't leave the coffin alone,
The cold winds catching up to me,
Whispering I'm on my own.

But I see you in the park,
On the streets, glaring at me,
The closer I get, the further you go,
May our proximity thrive in this distance,
It’s the only way I’ll survive.

From all my hundred fallacies,
You ought to be my favourite,
So deep into our infancy,
We sought to be our soulmates.

Looking back, you'll know,
In that moment,
What you lost
Can not be replaced.
But did you find
What you were looking for
In the spaces we left empty
Between our broken words?

Some days, it's harder to agree,
Amongst everything we fail to change,
There is a path to rearrange
In the exile of our thoughts
That often turn against us,
There is a blatant reality,
Waiting to unveil us.

There is a belonging
In the lush of the woods
Where the trees loom over us,
On a path
We decide for ourselves.
To the hills, it goes,
Till we're lost in the mist,
The dawn will come for us
And that night,
We'll be one before the morning sun.

Society,
It profits,
When you are told to man up,
When you are forced to be strong
And when you are shunned to feel,
There is a personna
Which is not wholly you,
You still put it before yourself
Even though it’s not true,
To this day you sing,
“You'll never walk alone.”
A little more belief
And you'll never be on your own.

Like a storm with no signal
But a sign from the universe,
We are where we belong,
Your hand in mine so tight,
Petrified of what might happen
If we leave it for sometime,
The horrors will come for us,
So now more than ever,
We need to be together,
Bare with me if I hold too tight,
I can't let go - it's so dark outside.

The past you wear
With immense pride
Was not a friend
But an enemy at sight.
It wasn't pleasant,
And sometimes it ate you alive
But you were born again
For another fight.

The thought of a world where love didn't exist,
Would hate still be
As vindictive as it is?

Diluted delusions

With such words we deceive ourselves,
The lies we tell and the truths we cover
All that's real,
We break into fragments
And pick the piece easiest to cope with,
Simplicity is ideal
But we prefer complication,
We don't wait for the night
To drink our diluted delusions.

Some voids in our heart
Stay hollow for a long time
Deprived of the blood, life and love.
It lost it’s cause when the chambers left empty
But didn’t stop beating
For the healing stays impending.

Forgotten anniversaries,
Rain check on dates,
Missed calls and voicemails
Are how much we speak.

Excuses are necessary,
Busy is so overused,
Often, we get creative
With another lousy excuse.

Stolen stares
And smirking at strangers,
The intent is never to hurt
But we too get distracted.

The time we meet
Is long overdue,
He gets me roses
Because he knows I adore blue.

Drowning in our realities,
We often dwell into a moment for so long,
It gets past us
And we’re still stuck there.

Failure is integral before undesirable.

With a halo, comes the burden of being half human,
The price we pay for our mortality,
Dignified we stand before all that is profane
But our lacking purity
Will make decadent graves.

"Let it stop before it starts."
- *Yashasvi Ghadale*

Why don't we stop before it starts?
The downfall, the end, the inevitable,
When the circle comes to an end,
Why do we still continue?
Why are we always in a dire need
To push the walls that close on us?
We cave in
And make the defeat the death of us.
Why not to be civil
And embrace the change brought to us.

The collapse is not the end of us.

Subterranean

Under layers lie our secrets,
Buried deep in the earth,
Each night, they crawl out
To write into our sanity.

Some are soothing to keep
And the others we dread to let go.
But in the midst of our hiding,
We forget the power time holds.

There is no secret left unsurfaced
And no revelation without devastation.

Such a curse is privilege,
It takes strength to be grateful,
A blind eye to all the beauty
And all eyes on what's beyond reach.

She wears a veil
To be guarded
But never to hide.
She chooses her battles,
Not all are meant to fight.
She takes the pain
To put you out of misery.
She makes mistakes,
They are so necessary.
She tries her best,
Puts her heart into things,
She knows it all,
Right from when it begins.

A fleeting shine in the extraordinary,
A timeless story within the mundane.
It will shine for as long as you watch
But the story, the narrative,
It'll last you a lifetime.

You were waving at the undone
From a distance you maintained,
Fled before the spark went out
Didn't wait for the end.

Goodbyes come easy to you
Because you never have to say it,
Stranded you leave them
Like it's in your blood to betray.

Sleep comes as peace in our early years
Till it becomes our rescue.
What is coming our way
Will get to us,
Then why does shutting our eyes
Feel like it will save us?

Before the sun sets

Lime white sheets with soft creases,
One leg outside and the other one trying to fit in with mine,
You slept for a while
But not wholly.
I could simply turn to look at you
And you'd already be staring into mine,
Half droopy, half in love,
Then the sun would come by
In all shades of golden,
Make those browns into something I could never defy.

That fleeting moment for the one last time,
The one before the final goodbye.

Sometimes a summer day
Isn't as sunny as it should be,
Could be covered in clouds
Without letting a ray escape
But when it's time for the sun to kiss goodbye,
It'll leave you with one beautiful sunset to remember.

All is given and all is forgiven,
For our blood, there be no boundaries,
The bonds remain forever,
Forlorn times ache for this warm love,
Without it, how long will you survive?

Gave into the fleeting moment,
It felt so right,
The righteousness you disregarded,
I saw it pass right through your eyes,
The love was ours,
We share the regret,
Your wrong was the doing
And mine was being your reason.

It is your essence that lingers
Long after you leave,
With me in my solitude,
You give me no time to grieve.
I know what follows
When I wake up next morning,
Your presence I hold on to
Becomes a memory I grow fond of.

We hide away
Than ask for a hand
From the people closest to us.

It is our burden, why bury them with it?

They are the only ones who will shoulder the pain
Without staging it to be a burden.
They'll do it time and again.
They'll do it till you're relieved,
Till you feel light,
Till you feel like yourself.

In shreds and less,
I gave you bits and parts.
In fragments and fractions,
I couldn't give you anymore.

Out of the greed of my heart,
There was only some to spare,
I gave you a conscious piece
And you left me an abundance.

The love that sparked my veins
Now I'm all out of it, emptied myself of it,
It was a fading feeling
And I'm watching it go
Like sand from my wrist,
It wasn't love anymore.

You brought me a souvenir when you went back to our past.
Nothing crystal, rather concrete - a lock to the door we feared closing,
Unhinged of us to have kept it open.
It was easy to go back but it took strength *to be back*,
A few last knocks before I begin to agree, all our love comes with an aching memory.

It's the days we count as blessings that help us through the tough ones.

Have you stared into a newborn's eyes?
They move frantically
Not because they are anxious
Because they want to see it all before it's time to blink again.
They see the world in frames, in moments,
The way it should be.
They understand the immediacy of being present,
Perhaps if not understand, it's innately known to them,
Until it's time to unlearn.

They've known it since the first brick fell weak. They heard the crunch, they saw the crack and encrusted it to be a part of the castle. Sullied every wall with the love they call a virtue. Such a disgrace is honoring this bond and worse, is to believe it’s true.

We want to be happy
But with happiness,
Follows a trail of sadness
And that is the undeniable law,
That is how nature equivates itself,
That is how we balance ourselves
In a manner unwanted but necessary.
What we truly want
Is a taste of peace
Without being stuck in the cycle,
Just plain days with love, gratitude
And faith - at consistent ease.

When did it get so hard?
Well, it was never easy,
We just didn't give enough credit to the struggles it brought
Even when we were fifteen.

My paper brings me power,
And my pen knights me to the occasion.
I scribble my thoughts,
Even the ones I can't assimilate into words,
In fragments, they remain
But concrete, they exist.
They fight with me when they have to
But pull their swords out when an outsider tries.
It's my battlefield,
And I will bleed in all the words I fail to write.

Have you wondered
How many bodies has your soul left?
Between unfinished chapters and untold apologies,
It haunts you another life.

Growing up, we never outgrow the child in us
Who sat through the days
Without knowing how dark they were,
A tiny hand that reaches out,
Carrying the burden of what shouldn’t have happened.
In all attempts to make you forget,
They do surface once in a while.
As gruesome it was,
You were just a child.

Merely relieving
Is to know
Even when I am lost
I'm still headed somewhere.

It’s the days, they look different.
Same as yesterday but not a month back.
They too age
And how sore it is to watch,
Unreal, how we believe
They’re as timeless as they seem,
How we pray they’ll always be
Those people that never leave.

Your calling,
Do you hear it?
It's screaming in your face right now
In frequencies beneath you
And it shall surface when you seek.
Spare no mercy for what you lose,
Your findings will be greater.
Devour every morsel of your passion
And wear it like your second skin,
There is no time for later.

Pain does not devour your soul,
It feeds on your wounds.
There is no joy or gratification,
Only agony, which it inflicts,
So imagine how much resides in itself,
To put you through it all.
It hasn't learnt to walk away yet
But it is not here to stay.

Your eyes melt away
For every day that passes by,
Wallowing in your tears,
Seeking comfort in what you fail to to defy.

Whenever I look into your eyes,
I see less of the love
That sparked us to be one
And I dread the day
This love reignites,
It won't be me
That brought you back to life.

Those we knew for years
Aren't with us today,
Our space has been replaced,
Our need has been erased
But a friend always stays,
Waiting for that day
When there'll be no better one
Than the one you knew yesterday.

To accept there's utter darkness around
Doesn't make us pessimists.
It's the very time we live in
That has reduced us to that mentality,
Seeking outside will do no good
Until you peek inside yourself,
You are throbbing with your light,
Make way for it to the world.

The walls are thin.

If you can hear my voice break,
I can hear you sob too.

There are walls between us.

We built them against the world but look at us now,
Built them too high - should we break them now?
Can we *please* break them now?

Let it reign and in succession you rise,
Your vice will level with your virtue,
Your whites will take a shade darker,
Be humbled by the lady in you
But embark on as,
Queen.

In a lacking attempt to love,
Quit forcing them for more,
Know when to stop,
For the right ones come by,
Your efforts won't go in vain,
They'll be matched.

It’s a curse on love
That every passionate romance
Ends in a tragedy,
There is an obsession
With being consumed by love
In which you go beyond bounds,
Lose yourself,
Take the fall,
And that is just the start of the wreckage.

She wears the sombres under her skin
And wears it like it was the piece missing.
Frail to her bones,
She thinks life is just this much,
Making peace with the worst
Was not the acceptance they talked about.

You don't get to decide who shares the same blood as you
But when you meet the people who do,
You realise
They've been with you for lives before this one.

Had you been there to see
The after-effects of your love,
Even the coldness of your heart
Wouldn't let you do it again.

Behind closed doors
Are some knuckles left bruised,
In a dying hope of a second chance,
They still knock
With regret in their arms.

There is something fatal
About a still photograph,
It doesn't take you back
But reminds you of the present,
What couldn't change
Is at the mercy of this moment,
Besides, everything that did
Is lost in time and space.

Probably the most beautiful things in life
Are the ones that are set free

From love, pain and mortality.

Years from now,
When we would've outdone our youth,
We'd still strive to be young at heart,
Watch our kids go old
And watch them grow apart.
Would they be by us,
Like we were by them,
Only time is the answer
And we have it in abundance,
Their best years are yet to come
And my last ones are yours to keep.

If we put down our hurting love,
I hope it reaches the heavens;
It will heal under the halos
Only to haunt us for some more.

The end, we never wish for it but it always falls upon us,
And sometimes we drag for it a little longer.
Often the break is beyond repair
And if we hold on to it, only we bleed.

The end, it doesn't have to be so undesirable.
Don't we beg for things to stop?
And the morning after it does, there's a taste of peace
that lingers in the air.

About The Author

Nidhi Shah, published her first book in an attempt to bring another lens on some heavily known themes.

Always keen on making something concrete out of her writing, this book allows her to bring her thoughts to a larger audience, previously bundled within years of journaling.

This book is entirely of what's around her so if she knows you, you're probably in these pages.

Writer's Pocket

Writer's Pocket is a publication house that first started out as an Instagram page on February 15th, 2016 by 2 college students. We began with the aim of providing a platform for amateur writers and budding poets.

As a publication house, we publish new anthologies of short stories, poems and other forms of writing every month. Every piece of content in our anthologies is submitted by young writers from all over India. We are completely unbiased in the selection process and try to provide the best content to our readers.

We have also published several novels and stand-alone collections of short writings by single authors. If you want to check out any of the books published by us, you can visit www.writerspocket.com or search for us on Amazon!

Also published by Writer's Pocket

Novels

In Search Of Home *by VK Mehta and Mahek Sharma*
Autumn - The Mosaic Of All *by Roobal Gupta*
Tangled Up In You *by Tanaya Atre*
In Search Of Spring *by Shreya Shively*
The Third Eye *by Nikhil Yadav*

Stand-alone books by single authors

The God Within *by Ratika Mishra*
The Flower Princess *by Sehrish Shadab*
Fiction With A Tinge Of Reality *by Shivangi Mandhiyan*
Highly Unstable *by Mayank*
Impressions *by Dr. Nidhi Kakkar*
Meraki *by Jayamadure S.*
Nazar *by Anierroodh Raammie (Hindi)*
Seeding Thoughts *by Shivangi Thaker*
Hallucinations *by Herat Udavat (Gujarati)*
I Know I Don't Know *by Sonali Sharma*
A Wallflower *by Arjun Deshmukh*
Dusk Dreams *by Kaavya S*
From The Sunflower's Heart *by Vanalika Vaid*
Saudade - The Presence In Absence *by Rashmi Nirvikar*
The Spring Cologne *by Yashaswini Angiras*
Dhi's Oracle of Divine Epiphanies *by Saudamini Mishra*
Fitoor *by Qabeera (Hindi)*
You Are Poetry *by S.V. Aurelia*
Silent Din *by Mohammed Sami Khan*
Brokenmoon *by maré vad raven*
Ignited Inspiration *by Anjali Patel*
Her: Chronicles of an un-warrior *by Monika Bhargava*